D0793420

DISCOVER THE
CONTINENTS

Australia

by Emily Rose Oachs

BLASTOFF!
3
READERS

BELLWETHER MEDIA • MINNEAPOLIS, MN

Note to Librarians, Teachers, and Parents:

Blastoff! Readers are carefully developed by literacy experts and combine standards-based content with developmentally appropriate text.

Level 1 provides the most support through repetition of high-frequency words, light text, predictable sentence patterns, and strong visual support.

Level 2 offers early readers a bit more challenge through varied simple sentences, increased text load, and less repetition of high-frequency words.

Level 3 advances early-fluent readers toward fluency through increased text and concept load, less reliance on visuals, longer sentences, and more literary language.

Level 4 builds reading stamina by providing more text per page, increased use of punctuation, greater variation in sentence patterns, and increasingly challenging vocabulary.

Level 5 encourages children to move from "learning to read" to "reading to learn" by providing even more text, varied writing styles, and less familiar topics.

Whichever book is right for your reader, Blastoff! Readers are the perfect books to build confidence and encourage a love of reading that will last a lifetime!

This edition first published in 2016 by Bellwether Media, Inc.

No part of this publication may be reproduced in whole or in part without written permission of the publisher. For information regarding permission, write to Bellwether Media, Inc., Attention: Permissions Department, 5357 Penn Avenue South, Minneapolis, MN 55419.

Library of Congress Cataloging-in-Publication Data

Oachs, Emily Rose.
 Australia / by Emily Rose Oachs.
    pages cm. – (Blastoff! Readers: Discover the Continents)
 Includes bibliographical references and index.
 Summary: "Simple text and full-color photography introduce beginning readers to Australia. Developed by literacy experts for students in kindergarten through third grade"– Provided by publisher.
 Audience: Grades K-3.
 ISBN 978-1-62617-326-2 (hardcover : alk. paper)
 1. Australia–Juvenile literature. I. Title.
 DU96.O33 2016
 994–dc23
                          2015028679

Printed in the United States of America, North Mankato, MN.

Table of Contents

The Smallest Continent

Sydney Harbour Bridge

Australia is the smallest **continent**. Its **area** is slightly smaller than the United States.

DID YOU KNOW?

- In Australia, summer begins in December and winter begins in June.

- The Outback covers much of Australia, but only 60,000 people live there.

- A huge rock in the Outback called Uluru is 5.8 miles (9.4 kilometers) around at its base!

- The Great Barrier Reef is the world's biggest coral reef system.

Great Barrier Reef

In Sydney, the Opera House and Harbour Bridge are famous **landmarks**. Shark Bay is along Australia's western coast. Many sea animals live in its waters.

Where Is Australia?

Australia is in the Southern and Eastern **hemispheres**. Water completely surrounds it. The Indian Ocean lies to Australia's west. To the east is the Pacific Ocean.

Small islands lie off Australia's coasts. The largest, Tasmania, is to the south.

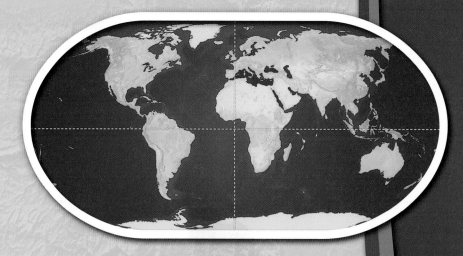

equator

Indian
Ocean

Pacific
Ocean

Australia

Tasmania

N
W E
S

The Land and Climate

Australian
Outback

Australia is mostly hot and dry. The **Outback** covers western and central Australia. This area has many deserts.

The Great Dividing
Range of mountains
rises along its eastern
coast. **Vast** grasslands
cover northern Australia.

grasslands

Great
Dividing Range

Australian
Outback

Great
Dividing Range

N
W · E
S

Tropical rain forests are found in northern Australia. Cooler rain forests trail down the eastern coast.

Great
Barrier Reef

Great
Barrier Reef

rain forests

N
W • E
S

The colorful Great Barrier Reef is off the northeastern coast. This long **coral reef** system was built up by many small **coral** skeletons.

eucalyptus forest

baobob tree

Daisies and other wildflowers bloom on the grasslands. In the deserts, acacia and baobob trees grow. Eucalyptus forests are found in eastern Australia.

In the tropical rain forests, **native** cherries and plums ripen. Waxflowers climb up trees.

waxflowers

plums

Many animals are found only in Australia. Kangaroos hop across the grasslands. Koalas and kookaburras sit in eucalyptus trees. In Australia's rivers, platypuses dive for food.

koala

kangaroo

kookaburra

platypus

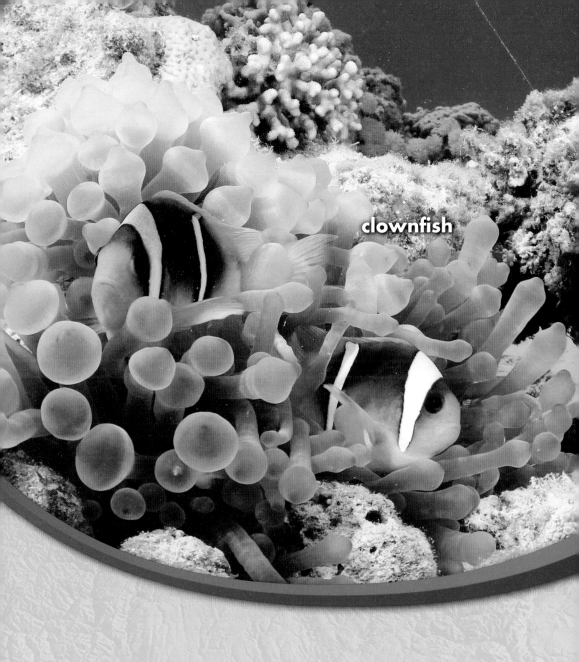

clownfish

Clownfish and angelfish swim through the Great Barrier Reef. Seahorses hide in the coral.

The People

Australia is the only continent that is a single country. It has six states and two **territories**. Nearly 23 million people live in Australia.

Most Australians live in cities along the coasts. Few people live in the Outback. However, many of Australia's native peoples make homes there.

Sydney is Australia's largest city. About 4.5 million people call it home.

Like many Australians, people in Sydney enjoy outdoor activities. They hike through national parks. In the ocean, they **snorkel** and surf. Australians value their continent's beautiful landscapes.

Fast Facts About Australia

Size: 2,970,000 square miles (7,700,000 square kilometers); smallest continent

Number of Countries: 1

Country: Australia

Number of People: 22.8 million people

Place with Most People: Sydney, Australia

Top Natural Resources: natural gas, iron, coal, gold, precious gems

Top Landmarks:
- Sydney Opera House (Sydney)
- Great Barrier Reef (northeastern coast)
- Uluru (Northern Territory)
- Shark Bay (western coast)

Uluru

Great
Barrier Reef

Shark Bay

Sydney

Sydney
Opera House

N
W E
S

Glossary

area—a region's size

continent—one of the seven main land areas on Earth; the continents are Africa, Antarctica, Asia, Australia, Europe, North America, and South America.

coral—a small ocean animal whose skeleton makes up a coral reef

coral reef—a structure made of coral that usually grows in shallow seawater

hemispheres—halves of the globe; the equator and prime meridian divide Earth into different hemispheres.

landmarks—important structures or places

native—originally from a specific place

Outback—the large, inland area of Australia where few people live

snorkel—to swim using a tube to breathe underwater

territories—areas of land that belong to a country

tropical rain forests—thick, green forests that lie in the hot and wet regions near the equator

vast—broad or large

To Learn More

AT THE LIBRARY

Bodden, Valerie. *Great Barrier Reef*. Mankato, Minn.: Creative Education, 2010.

Meister, Cari. *Do You Really Want to Meet a Platypus?* Mankato, Minn.: Amicus Illustrated, 2015.

Niz, Xavier. *Spotlight on Australia*. Mankato, Minn.: Capstone Press, 2011.

ON THE WEB

Learning more about Australia is as easy as 1, 2, 3.

1. Go to www.factsurfer.com.

2. Enter "Australia" into the search box.

3. Click the "Surf" button and you will see a list of related web sites.

With factsurfer.com, finding more information is just a click away.

Index

The images in this book are reproduced through the courtesy of: Simon Bradfield, front cover; Taras Vyshnya, p. 4; tororo reaction, p. 5; kawhia, p. 8; Leah-Anne Thompson, p. 9; Johan Larson, p. 10; Pete Niesen, p. 11; Kitch Bain, p. 12 (top); Adwo, p. 12 (bottom); happytotakephoto, p. 13 (top); D. Parer & E. Parer-Cook/ Minden Pictures/ Corbis, p. 13 (bottom); Natalia Fadosova, p. 14 (left); Lev Kropotov, p. 14 (top right); Birdiegal, p. 14 (center right); worldswildlifewonders, p. 14 (bottom right); Rich Carey, p. 15; Ida Jarosova, p. 16; RosaIreneBetancourt 7/ Alamy, p. 18; artincamera, p. 19; Peter Zurek, p. 21 (top left); Edward Haylan, p. 21 (top right); Monica Johansen, p. 21 (bottom left); Aleksandar Todorovic, p. 21 (bottom right).